# The Art of
# GIFT WRAPPING

# The Art of
# GIFT WRAPPING

ALEXANDRA EAMES AND CAROL SPIER

*Photography by Bill Milne*

SMITHMARK

**A FRIEDMAN GROUP BOOK**

This edition published in 1993 by SMITHMARK Publishers Inc.
16 East 32nd Street, New York NY 10016

ISBN 0-8317-3860-X

*The Art of Gift Wrapping*
was prepared and produced by
Michael Friedman Publishing Group, Inc.
15 West 26th Street
New York, NY 10010

Editor: Nathaniel Marunas
Art Director: Jeff Batzli
Designer: Tanya Ross-Hughes
Photography Director: Christopher C. Bain

Typeset by Classic Type
Printed in Hong Kong and bound in China by Leefung-Asco Printers Ltd.

All gift wraps in this book were generously provided by ©Stephen Lawrence, Carlstadt, NJ

SMITHMARK Books are available for bulk purchase for sales promotion and premium use.
For details write or call the manager of special sales, SMITHMARK Publishers Inc.,
16 East 32nd Street, New York, NY 10016; (212) 532-6600.

## ACKNOWLEDGMENTS

*The authors would like to thank Lisa Soicher and her staff at Stephen Lawrence for their help and for providing the gift wraps, ribbons, and papers used in this book.*

# CONTENTS

# HOW TO USE THE DIRECTIONS IN THIS BOOK

*General directions are given on this page for making a basic seamless wrap and on the opposite page for a keepsake wrap (where the top of the box is wrapped separately from the bottom). Directions for making a multi-loop or twist bow are given on page 11. Directions for creating coordinated gift tags are also supplied on page 11. You can of course interpret any of the gift wraps shown by using any number of papers, colors, or seasonal schemes. The materials used for each wrap are identified by type, color, or pattern, but you should feel free to substitute materials of your choice, and to adjust the proportions of the trims so they are appropriate to the size of your package.*

## WORKING WITH TISSUE PAPER

Tissue paper comes in many wonderful colors and patterns. It is fragile, but not difficult to work with if handled carefully. If tissue paper is creased from the package you can press it with a common steam iron. It is a good idea to give your package an underwrapping of one or more layers of white tissue paper before covering it with the decorative tissue—this renders the wrap opaque and softens the edges of the gift so that the paper is less likely to tear.

## BASIC SUPPLIES

It is assumed that anyone wrapping gifts will have basic art supplies on hand, so only those tools that are unusual are listed with the materials needed for a particular wrap. You will use pencils, scissors, rulers (the transparent grid-marked kind is useful), white glue, rubber cement, transparent and double-stick tape, floral wire, wire cutters, and an iron frequently, so collect them before you begin.

## Seamless Wrap

*This is the classic way to wrap a box, and it is very easy. If your paper has a stripe, pronounced pattern, or motif, take the time to position it appropriately on your box—aligned with the edge, centered, or symmetrically spaced as desired. If you seal your wrap with double-stick tape it will look more profes-sional; if this tape is not available, use high-quality transparent tape.*

*If you are not familiar with this technique, read through the directions and then try a sample wrap to judge the effect.*

**1.** You will need a piece of paper that is large enough to go around your box with a slight over-lap and with an amount extending beyond each end that is about 1″ longer than the thickness of the box. (The paper can extend by as little as half the thickness of the box plus a turning margin; in this case, points will form on the box ends.) Wrap your box loosely with paper to estimate how much you will need, and cut a piece that is sufficiently large. Remember, you can always trim any excess paper, but you cannot add on to a piece that is too small.

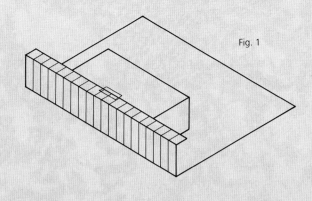

Fig. 1

**3.** Fold the margin up over the side, creasing it along the top and bottom edges of the box. Tape it to the bottom of the box. (See Fig. 1)

**4.** Fold the paper extending beyond the opposite edge of the box up and over in the same manner. Hold it so that it overlaps the paper already taped to the box. Fold excess paper to the wrong side so that there is an overlap. (See Fig. 2)

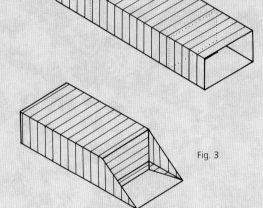

Fig. 2

**5.** Let the paper unwrap so that it is flat on the table again, and sharpen the fold made in the last step. Trim any excess if the margin folded to the wrong side is more than 1/2″ wide. Put some double-stick tape on the margin, wrap the paper over the box again, and press in place.

**6.** Be sure that the side of the box with the taped seam is facing upwards. Gently fold the paper at one end of the box downward over the edge. A folded triangle of paper will form at each side of the box. With your fingers, crease the folds of those triangles and the fold that forms where the excess paper meets the paper extending from under the box. You can carefully trim the excess paper beyond this fold if you like. (See Fig. 3)

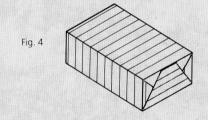

Fig. 3

**7.** Fold the triangle at each side edge onto the end of the box and crease the diagonal lines that form on the remaining paper that extends from under the box. You can tape the triangles to the box if they don't stay in place by themselves.

**8.** Fold the remaining paper up onto the end of the box. Crease it lightly where it meets the upper edge, then unfold it and sharpen the crease. Trim the folded margin if necessary, and put some double-stick tape on it. Fold it back onto the end of the box and press to secure. (See Fig. 4)

Repeat steps 6, 7, and 8 at the other end of the box.

Fig. 4

**2.** Place the paper wrong side up on a table. Put the box on it, upside down, with one long edge of the box centered on one side edge of the paper. (If the box is square, the paper should be square, too.) Slide the box away from the edge of the paper until there is a margin of paper deep enough to cover the side and lap onto the bottom of the box.

# Keepsake Wrap

*The bottom and top of a keepsake wrap are covered separately, making the (now recyclable) box an integral part of the gift. Making a keepsake wrap is no more difficult than making a seamless one, but it takes a little longer. You can cover the top and bottom of your box with the same paper, or use contrasting colors or patterns. Some enameled or slick-surfaced papers are difficult to use for this technique—especially if the box is large—because they crease so easily. Tissue paper is not really durable enough for a box that is intended for reuse.*

### TO COVER THE TOP

**1.** Place the paper wrong side up on a table. Place the top of the box upside down on the paper. Cut a piece of paper that extends beyond each side of the box top far enough to wrap up and over the edge.

**2.** Center the top of the box upside down on the paper. If you like, you can attach the top of the box to the paper with double-stick tape; this makes it a little easier to complete the next steps. Fold up the paper on two opposite sides (the longer sides if your box is rectangular). Crease the folds, and double-stick the paper to the sides of the box (if necessary).

**3.** Fold the paper extending beyond one end of the box top around the side corners, creasing the diagonal folds that form on the paper extending from under the box. Tape the paper to the ends of the box top. Repeat for the opposite end of the box top.

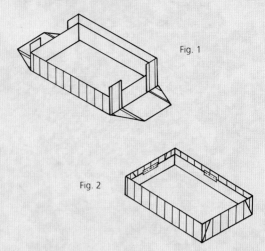

Fig. 1

Fig. 2

**4.** Gently fold the paper extending above the sides to the inside of the box; you may find it helpful to cut partway into the margin above each corner so that you can fold in one edge at a time. Tape the paper to the inside of the box. (See Fig. 1)

**5.** Fold the paper at one end of the box up and over the edge, and tape it in place. Repeat for the opposite end. (See Fig. 2)

## TO COVER THE BOTTOM OF THE BOX

**(Note: If the box is shallow, you can cover it in the same way you covered the top. However, if the box is deep, or if your paper has a stripe or one-way design, you will achieve better results if you cover it as follows.)**

**1.** Measure the height of the box bottom. Measure the width of the box bottom (the shorter direction, if the box is rectangular), divide the measurement in half, and add this number to the height; add about 3″ more for folding margins. This is the height of the paper you will need. Measure the distance around the box and add about 2″ for folding margins. This is the width of the paper you will need.

**2.** Cut a piece of paper to the measurements determined in the last step, with the pattern arranged as desired. It may be necessary to piece several widths of the paper to keep the pattern oriented as you wish; in this case, fold the additional pieces under the overlapping edge and match the pattern.

**3.** Place the paper wrong side up on the table. Place the box on its side on the paper, with the top edge of the paper extending about 2 1/2″ beyond the open edge of the box, and one side edge of the paper extending 1″ beyond one side edge of the box.

**4.** Fold the 1″ margin up onto the side of the box, crease the fold, and tape the margin to the box. (See Fig. 3)

**5.** Wrap the paper extending beyond the other side of the box up and over the remaining sides. Hold it so that it overlaps the paper already taped to the box and crease it lightly along that edge of the box.

**6.** Let the paper unwrap so that it is flat on the table again, and sharpen the crease made in the last step. Cut off any excess paper if the margin folded to the wrong side is more than 1/2″ wide. Put some double-stick tape on the margin, wrap the paper over the box again, and press in place.

**7.** If the box is rectangular, place it on the table with one of the longer sides facing upward. Gently fold the paper at the bottom of the box downward over the edge. A folded triangle of paper will form at each side edge of the box. With your fingers, crease the folds of these triangles.

**8.** Fold the triangle at each side edge onto the bottom of the box and crease the diagonal lines that form on the remaining paper that extends from under the box. You can tape the triangles to the box if they don't stay in place by themselves. (See Fig. 4)

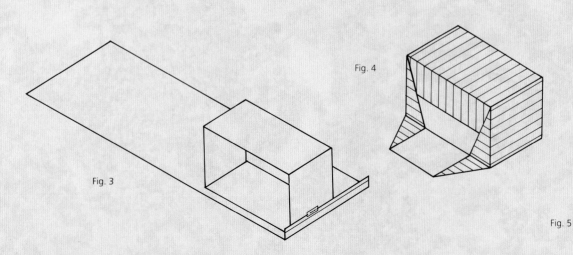

Fig. 3

Fig. 4

Fig. 5

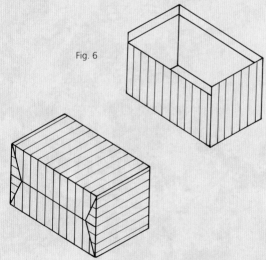

Fig. 6

**9.** Fold the remaining paper up onto the bottom of the box. Crease it lightly where it overlaps the piece folded down from the upper edge, unfold it, and sharpen the crease. Trim the folded margin if necessary, and put some double-stick tape on it. Fold it back onto the end of the box and press to secure. (See Fig. 5)

**10.** Place the box upright on the table. Gently fold the paper extending above the sides and ends to the inside of the box; you may find it helpful to cut partway into the margin above each corner so that you can fold in one edge at a time. Tape the paper to the inside of the box. (See Fig. 6)

# Multi-Loop or Twist Bow

*The type of ribbon you choose for a multi-loop bow affects the character of the finished bow. Woven-edged cloth ribbons make soft lush bows; non-woven and stiffened cloth ribbons make crisp ones. Wire-edged ribbons make bows that are easy to manipulate and can be very lush, but they do not have the soft or floppy look of other woven ribbon bows. The width of the ribbon will also affect the appearance of the bow, and unless you wish to make a very small bow, very narrow ribbons are not recommended for this technique. Multi-loop bows require a lot of ribbon, so plan accordingly.*

*The directions that follow will make a bow that is about 5" in diameter. You can make a larger or*

*smaller bow by wrapping the ribbon around a larger or smaller piece of cardboard. You can make a more generous bow by wrapping the ribbon around the cardboard a few extra times.*

**1.** Cut a 2" x 5" piece of cardboard. Place the end of the ribbon about 3" from one end (so that it overlaps the midpoint) and wrap the ribbon around the cardboard five times, overlapping the midpoint again; cut the excess.

**2.** If you are using a cloth ribbon, tack the end of the ribbon to the loop beneath it with a needle and thread. If you are using a non-woven ribbon, secure the end with tape.

**3.** Slide the ribbon off the cardboard, maintaining the wrapped loop. Cut a small V-shaped notch about 1/3 of the way in from each edge through all layers at the midpoint, as shown in the illustration. If you are using wire-edged ribbon, do not cut any notches, but pinch the edges together at the midpoint.

**4.** Wrap another piece of ribbon, or a piece of floral wire, around the bow at the midpoint, and tie or twist to secure. If you have left tails of ribbon on your package, you can use them for this purpose, but it is easier to handle the bow if it is tied separately; wire will make the least bulky center, and if you leave some excess it can be used to attach the bow to the package.

**5.** Pull the loops of the bow out one at a time, twisting them against the binding in the center.

**6.** Attach the bow to the package.

# Coordinating Gift Tags

*Gift tags of all shapes, sizes and colors can be made from standard cardboard tags sold in stationery and office supply stores. Covered with gift wrap or tissue paper and trimmed to a new shape you can coordinate the tag with any package. A hole punch provides a clean hole large enough for a colorful ribbon or cord tie.*

*To cover the tag with gift wrap paper or ribbon you will need paper-backed fusible web (an iron-on bonding web) or rubber cement. The iron-on web takes a little longer and requires the use of a steam iron but is neater than cement. Plastic-based ribbons and some foil papers will melt under the iron and require the use of rubber cement. Place the cardboard tag on the paper side of the web and trace it with a pencil. Cut out along the marked outline. Place the cutout web with the protective paper side up on the tag and iron it in place. Remove the protective paper backing. Lay a larger piece of gift wrap paper on the tab and iron it. Trim away the excess paper with sharp scissors. If desired, you may trim the tag into a new shape. With the hole punch, make a larger hole and tie in place with a piece of ribbon or cord.*

# CLAM SHELL JEWELRY BOX

*Gilded clam shells make pretty and unusual keepsake boxes, perfect for jewelry or other small treasures. You will need a whole clam shell for each box. Mismatched halves you might pick up on the beach will not fit together neatly; if you do not live near a beach, ask your seafood vendor for a hard-shell clam about 3″ across. Steam it till it opens, then eat or discard the clam. Scrub out the shell (with a little bleach if odor persists) and allow it to dry. Clam shells can also be obtained through mail-order shell supply catalogs.*

**1.** Following the manufacturer's directions, gild the outside of the shells with gold leaf. When dry, gild the inside of the shells with silver, letting the natural purple color remain at the edges.

**2.** Fold the grosgrain ribbon in half, widthwise. Spread some craft glue on the inside edge of each half of the shell where the hinge was (the flat area to one side of the notched edge).

Place the grosgrain on the glue on one shell, with the fold extending about 1/4″ beyond the edge, and top with the other shell; make sure the ribbon does not interfere with the closure. Let the new hinge dry enough to be safely handled.

**3.** Open the shells and glue the tails of ribbon inside, trimming excess as necessary. Let dry completely. Rub ribbon with leaf if desired.

## YOU WILL NEED

- 1 pair of clam shells, cleaned and with the hinge removed

- Synthetic gold and silver leaf

- 18″ piece of silver gift tying cord

- Scrap of 1″-wide white grosgrain ribbon for hinge

**4.** Referring to the photograph, place a thin line of glue across the outside of one shell and press the cord into it, leaving sufficient length to tie the cord beyond the open edge of the shell and to wrap and tie beyond the hinged edge. Let dry completely. Turn the shell over, fold the cord loosely over the hinge, and glue to the other side in the same manner. Let dry completely.

**5.** Tie the cord in a square knot to close your shell box, then tie a simple knot on each tail and trim the excess. Dip the raw ends of the cord in glue to prevent fraying.

# GLITTER BOXES

*Sparkling glitter in lots of colors can decorate a plain keepsake box, an exciting package for jewelry, or other small treasures. For a perfectly smooth surface or an unusual background color, the box and lid may be wrapped with solid-colored gift paper. Follow the directions for keepsake boxes on page 9. Fill the box with a nest of shining tinsel to protect the gift and to make a nice surprise when the box is opened.*

## YOU WILL NEED

• Glitter in assorted colors   • Solid-colored gift paper   • Small watercolor paintbrush

**1.** Spread glue for each color area separately. Use a paintbrush and glue diluted with water for broad areas and the pointed nozzle top of the glue container to draw thin lines. Sprinkle the glitter into the wet glue and shake the excess onto a clean sheet of paper. Work on small areas one at a time so the glue does not dry. By keeping the colors separate, you can return the excess glitter to its original container.

**2.** Repeat the process for each color. Use enough glue to get good glitter coverage. Bare spots can be touched up with additional glue and glitter.

# FABRIC WRAPS

*This is a festive and easy way to wrap any cubic, cylindrical, or pillar-shaped object; it is ideal for jars or cans of food, or thick candles. Crisp fabrics will give the jauntiest tails to the outer wrap, while heavy fabrics will not tie as nicely. Read the first step of the directions to figure the approximate dimensions of fabric needed for your gift.*

**1.** Measure the complete distance around the height of your gift from the center of the bottom over the top and back to the center of the bottom; note this measurement. The fabric for the inner-wrap square should be this measurement from corner to diagonally opposite corner; fabric for the outer-wrap rectangle should be this measurement-plus-20" long and this measurement (but not more than 18") wide; and fabric for the tie should be this measurement-plus-15" long and 3" wide.

**2.** If desired, fringe the ends of the tie and outer-wrap fabrics. Use a pin to loosen the crosswise threads one by one and pull them away.

**3.** Place the inner wrap wrong side up on a table. Center the gift, top down, on the fabric; pull each corner to the bottom of the gift and tape to secure. Turn the gift right side up and tuck in any extending wings of fabric so they lie between gift and wrap.

**YOU WILL NEED**

Three pieces of contrasting or coordinating fabric:

- one square for inner wrap

- one rectangle for outer wrap

- one strip (1"-wide ribbon will work) for tie

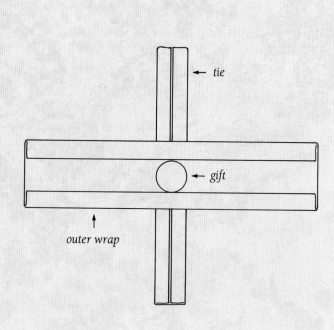

← tie

← gift

↑
outer wrap

**4.** Press both long edges of the tie to the center of the wrong side, forming a strip 1/2" wide.

**5.** Place the tie wrong side up on table, perpendicular to the edge. Place the outer wrap wrong side up on top of it, with the long edges parallel to the table edge and the centers of the wrap and tie aligned. Loosely fold about 3" to the wrong side along each long edge of the outer wrap (see illustration).

**6.** Place the gift right side up on the intersection of the outer wrap and tie. Lift the ends of the tie and tie in a square knot on top of the gift.

**7.** Keeping long edges folded up, lift the ends of the outer wrap and tie in a square knot on top of the gift. With your fingers, arrange the outer-wrap fabric to drape evenly on each side of the tie, and adjust the tails on top as necessary.

# FLOWERPOT COVER

*Plant gifts are always difficult to wrap, but since you are likely to be giving them to thank a hostess or wish someone well, you need not conceal them as long as you make the presentation festive. Here is an easy way to dress up a flowerpot. Paper with an obvious directional pattern (such as stripes or plaid) is not suitable. Your pot should be empty while you make the pattern.*

**1.** Draw a line from top to bottom on the flowerpot. Place the pot on its side on scrap paper. With the line adjacent to the paper; draw a corresponding line on the paper. Holding a pencil at the rim, roll the pot over the paper to mark the top shape, rolling until the line on the side meets the paper again. Draw another corresponding line on the paper.

Move the pencil to the bottom of the pot and roll the pot back over the paper, marking the bottom shape. Lift the pot and, adding 1/2″ at top and bottom and 1″ at each end, cut out the pattern.

**2.** Wrap the pattern around the pot with 1/2″ extending at the top and bottom edges to check fit. Adjust if necessary.

**3.** Position the pattern on the gift wrap, centering any pattern motif as desired, and mark and cut out the cover.

## YOU WILL NEED

• Scrap paper for pattern

• Flowerpot

• Patterned wrapping paper

• Paper-backed fusible web (optional)

• Floral wire for plant embellishments

**4.** On the wrong side of the cover, mark a line 1/2″ from the bottom edge. With scissors, clip through the margin to the line at 1/2″ intervals. Fold the clipped edge to the wrong side and crease the curve. Fold 1/2″ on one straight edge to the wrong side.

**5.** Put the wrong side of the cover against the pot (with plant inside), with the bottom edges aligned. Roll the cover around the pot. Tape the straight-cut edge of the cover to the pot. Lap the folded edge of the cover over it and secure with double-stick tape.

**6.** If using gift wrap with motifs (such as butterflies shown), cut them in pairs from the wrap. Using rubber cement or fusible web, glue the pairs together, right sides out, inserting a piece of floral wire in each. See the directions for making gift tags on page 11. (If the motifs are not symmetrical, glue each to the wrong side of plain paper, then cut out along the outer edge.) Position the motifs in the foliage and secure with the wires.

# WINTER WHITE FEATHERS AND TWIGS

*In this wrap, white painted twigs and feathers are reflected in the icelike surface of silver foil paper. This wrapping is quick, easy, and dramatic; use it for Christmas or a seasonal birthday gift.*

## YOU WILL NEED

• White-painted twigs   • Feathers   • Silver foil gift paper   • Silver or white satin ribbon   • Hot glue sticks and a glue gun

**1.** Wrap the box according to the directions for seamless wrap on page 8 or keepsake wrap on page 9.

**2.** Spread newspaper on the work surface to protect it.

**3.** Cut twigs to the desired length and glue stems together in a bunch. Glue the bottom tips of the feathers to the stems at the same spot. Tie a bow (see page 11 for bow directions) and hot glue it to the feathers and twigs.

**4.** Wrap the ribbon around the package on the diagonal, then cut and tape the ends at one corner. The taped cut ends will be covered with the twigs and bow. Hot glue the twigs and bow to the package.

# CYLINDRICAL CONTAINER

*Recycle an empty oatmeal container by covering it with decorative paper and filling it with cookies or trinkets, or use it as shown here as a way to present small kitchen utensils for a shower or housewarming. For fun, select decorative paper that reflects the theme of the gift, and embellish the wrap with ribbon.*

**1.** Trace around the bottom of the container onto tissue paper. Cut out the circle and affix to the bottom of the container with double-stick tape.

**2.** Wrap the container with tissue paper, leaving 3/4" extending at lower edge and 6" extending at upper edge. Secure overlap with tape.

**3.** With scissors, clip the lower margin and fold onto the bottom of the container; secure with tape.

**4.** Measure the height and circumference of the container, then add 1" to each measurement. Cut a rectangle of decorative paper to these dimensions.

**5.** On the wrong side of the rectangle, draw a line 3/4" from the top edge, place the edge of a ruler along this line, and fold and crease paper over it. Repeat for the lower edge. In the same manner, make a fold 1/2" from one of the ends.

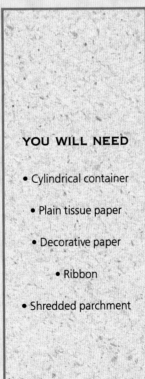

## YOU WILL NEED

- Cylindrical container

- Plain tissue paper

- Decorative paper

- Ribbon

- Shredded parchment

**6.** Center the rectangle between the top and bottom of the cylinder; tape the cut edge to the tissue. Wrap the paper around the cylinder, overlapping the folded edge and securing it with double-stick tape.

**7.** For each spoon or other utensil you plan to wrap, cut a 12" square of colored tissue paper. Fold the square in half horizontally. Insert the utensil between the layers at one end, with the bowl toward the fold. Loosely roll the tissue around the utensil, folding back the final layer, and pinch the tissue around the handle; wrap and tie with ribbon to secure.

**8.** Fill the container with shredded parchment and insert the utensils.

# EMBROIDERY FLOSS AND TISSUE WRAP

*Embroidery floss is widely available in small skeins in many colors that can be combined with layers of different colored tissue paper for a delicate Japanese look. The tiny knots with short tufts of thread are most appropriate on small gift boxes or soft packages such as rolled-up socks. The tag is covered with lavender tissue paper.*

## YOU WILL NEED

• Six-strand embroidery floss, silk or cotton   • Colored tissue wrapping paper

**1.** Wrap the box or package in tissue paper according to the instructions for seamless wrap on page 8. For an interesting texture combine two different layers in different colors, such as pale pink over shocking pink or purple.

**2.** Tie embroidery floss, using all six strands, around the package, knot it, and cut off the ends about 1/4″ from the knot. Repeat with many strands in many colors.

# PRESSED FLOWER WRAP

*Pressed flowers are too beautiful to waste on a throwaway wrap, so apply them to a covered keepsake box or arrange them in such a way that the paper can be salvaged and framed. For best results, choose a sturdy uncoated paper (such as the matte-finish recycled wrap shown) that will absorb diluted craft glue. If you have never worked with pressed flowers, make a small sample to see how they handle. Pressed flowers are fragile and easily blown out of position, so avoid wearing billowy or bulky clothes while you make this wrap.*

**1.** Wrap the box following the directions for the keepsake wrap on page 9.

**2.** Arrange the flowers on the top of the box as desired. You will have to remove any overlapping flowers in order to glue the underlayer in place, so if you have a Polaroid camera, take a photograph of the arrangement to aid you while you work; otherwise lightly mark flower placement with a pencil.

**3.** Squeeze a small amount of craft glue into the bowl. Dilute it with a few drops of water and mix to the consistency of heavy cream.

## YOU WILL NEED

- Sturdy box with separate lid

- Plain paper

- Assorted pressed flowers and leaves

- Bowl for glue

- Small soft paintbrush

- Toothpick

**4.** If necessary, remove any flowers that lie on top of others, and set aside. Then, working with one piece at a time, lift a flower and brush the back with diluted glue, return the flower to position and press gently in place. (Use the toothpick to dot glue onto the back of tiny or slender sections, or to slide additional glue under an area that is not properly affixed. If you inadvertently smear the glue, blot it very gently with a small piece of damp paper towel.)

**5.** In the same manner, glue and reposition any top flowers removed for the previous step.

#  FELT HEART TIE

*Plump red hearts with pinked edges will dress up gifts for Valentine's Day or any other heartfelt occasion. Attached to a length of satin cord, the hearts can be worn as a necklace, hung on a Christmas tree, or used as mini-pincushions if given with a gift of sewing notions.*

## YOU WILL NEED

• Scraps of red felt • Pinking shears • Kraft paper for the pattern • Red embroidery (six-strand) floss

• Red satin gift cord • Sewing needle • Polyester fiberfill

**1.** To make a heart-shaped pattern cut a 2″ square of craft paper and fold it in half. With the fold as the center, draw half a heart shape and cut it out. Unfold the pattern.

**2.** Pin the pattern to two layers of felt. Cut out the heart shape with pinking shears.

**3.** With embroidery floss and a sharp embroidery needle, sew running stitches 1/4″ inside the edge of the heart, leaving an opening on one side for stuffing. Do not tie off the floss.

**4.** Stuff the heart with fiberfill and continue stitching to close the opening. Secure thread and trim ends.

**5.** Repeat steps 2 through 4 for the second heart.

**6.** Wrap the package according to the directions for seamless wrap on page 8. Wrap the satin cord around the package, tie it loosely to determine its finished length, and cut it.

**7.** Sew a heart to each end of the cord, using three strands of floss and a small sharp needle. Tie the cord around the package and add a name tag if desired.

# TISSUE PAPER COLLAGE

*Tissue paper comes in many wonderful colors, and because it is translucent, it can be arranged in a collage to make even more colors. This is a great way to use up scraps of paper, and you can arrange them in a random pattern, as shown, or create a picture; the resulting paper is remarkably sturdy. Dressmaker's fusible web was the bonding agent for this gift wrap; if you don't have an iron you can use diluted craft glue, but it is not as convenient to use.*

## YOU WILL NEED

• Sheet of white tissue paper in size needed to wrap gift  • Assorted colored tissue paper, cut into 8" squares

• Paper-backed fusible web cut in 7 1/2" squares  • Ribbon

**1.** Following the manufacturer's directions, fuse the transfer web to the colored tissue squares. Remove the paper backing from each, and note which side has the web (it will feel pebbly).

**2.** Press the white tissue paper.

**3.** Tear the colored tissue into small pieces and arrange them, a few at a time, glue side down, on the white tissue. Fuse in place.

**4.** Continue in this manner until the white tissue is covered with colored tissue; pass your iron over a piece of paper towel from time to time to remove any glue that might seep through the tissue.

**5.** Wrap the box and finish with a simple bow. Fuse or glue a scrap of the collage to a gift tag and trim any excess from the edges.

# CHAMPAGNE BOTTLE AND TWO FLUTES

*This smashing presentation to help usher in the New Year also ensures that the bottle and two glasses arrive safely. The base of the bottle and the glasses are tightly wedged in a shallow box with packing paper. A liberal covering of gold tinsel covers the packing and adds festive sparkle. The glasses take on more glitter with glued-on moon and star confetti. (The rubber cement can be washed off later.)*

## YOU WILL NEED

• Small carton large enough to hold the bases of a bottle and two glasses   • Utility knife   • Skewer or darning needle

• Mirror confetti in star and moon shapes (or conventional squares and circles)   • Mirror wrap or plain tissue paper   • Curling ribbon

• Brown kraft paper or a crumpled paper bag for packing   • Shredded gold tinsel strands

**1.** With the utility knife, cut down the sides of the carton to measure 3 1/4" high.

**2.** With a skewer or darning needle, place dots of rubber cement on the outside of one champagne glass. Sprinkle mirror confetti in the wet cement. Repeat for the other glass.

**3.** Wrap the champagne bottle in two layers of mirror wrap or tissue by placing it in the center of the wrap and pulling the corners up around the neck of the bottle. Tie a piece of ribbon around the neck to hold the wrap in place. Tie two or three additional bows to the neck of the bottle and curl the ends of the ribbon.

**4.** Place the bottle and two glasses in the carton and pack the brown kraft paper around the bases so they cannot tip over or slide about. Spread the gold tinsel over the packing and tuck it in around the edge of the box.

# WIRE BASKET WRAP

*When you use a basket instead of a box as a package, it becomes part of the gift. Fill it with items for a housewarming or shower gift, and choose colors that suit the occasion. Follow these directions or interpret them for your own basket.*

## YOU WILL NEED

• Wire basket large enough to hold gift   • White and yellow tissue paper (or colors desired)   • White and mint narrow curling ribbon (or colors desired)

**1.** Cut the green ribbon into lengths sufficient to tie bows as desired. Tie bows around the top of basket.

**2.** Cut the green ribbon into lengths sufficient to make a curling fringe. Fold each length in half, thread the fold from front to back to front behind the horizontal wire, then pass the cut ends through the folded end; pull tight to secure over the wire and curl the ends.

**3.** Measure the total diameter of the basket (twice the depth plus the distance across). Cut two squares of yellow tissue paper this size. Place one over the other with corners alternating, and line the basket with them.

**4.** Cut two squares of white tissue paper large enough to enclose your gift. Place one over the other with their corners alternating (forming an eight-pointed star). Place the gift in the center, pull the corners up over it, pinch them together, and tie with the green ribbon to secure. Place the gift in the lined basket.

# PARTY POPPER TUBE WRAP

*A cardboard tube is often the best way to protect a fragile gift. Prints, posters, and maps come to mind first but many other gifts, such as scarves, cooking utensils, knives, and even a writing pen or paintbrushes, could be packed in tubes. Paper towels, wrapping paper, toilet tissue, and oatmeal box tubes can all be cut down to the desired length for popper-style wrappings.*

## YOU WILL NEED

• Tissue paper and/or gift wrap paper • Cardboard tube • Brown kraft paper or paper bag • Curling ribbon • Self-stick premade bows

**1.** Wrap the gift in tissue paper and insert it into the tube. Add some crumpled kraft paper to each end of the tube to prevent the gift from slipping out.

**2.** Cut three squares of tissue paper for each end of the tube. These pieces can be 1' square for a large tube and smaller for smaller tubes. Gather and twist the center of each square and tape it to the inside of the end of the tube. Tape three pieces around the perimeter of each end of the tube.

**3.** Cut lengths of thin curling ribbon in three or four colors. Pull all the colors off their spools at the same time and tape the ends together. Insert the taped ends into the ends of the tube and tape in place. Curl the ends of some of the ribbons.

**4.** Measure the length of the tube and cut a piece of wrapping paper 6" longer and wide enough to wrap around the tube. Cut a 3" fringe on each end of the paper. (This fringe can be shorter for shorter tubes.) Wrap the paper around the tube, fold the cut edge under 1/2" and tape in place.

**5.** Decorate the tissue paper with tiny self-stick bows.

# PATCHWORK BOX TOP

*Anyone who quilts would love to receive a keepsake with a paper patchwork pattern glued to the top. Whether you use the pattern provided or one of your own favorites, take the time to plan its arrangement on your box, and select patterned papers with sufficient contrast.*

**1.** Wrap box following directions for the keepsake wrap on page 9.

**2.** Cut a piece of graph paper the same size as the box top. Find the midpoint of each side, and draw perpendicular lines crossing at the center.

**3.** Trace the patchwork motif and cut it out along its perimeter. Arrange it, as shown, on the graph paper (leave 3/4" between adjacent motifs), or as suits your box. If the motif does not fit comfortably, redraft it on another piece of graph paper, or enlarge or reduce it on a photocopier.

**4.** Draw around each motif to mark its position on the graph paper. Cut each outlined motif from the graph paper, leaving a template with six openings.

**5.** Place the template on the box top and outline each opening lightly with pencil. Remove the template.

**6.** Cut the tracing paper motif apart to make patterns for the patchwork, keeping one piece of each shape.

## YOU WILL NEED

- Sturdy rectangular box with separate lid

- Graph paper

- Tracing paper

- Contrasting plain and printed papers to cover top and bottom of box

- Scraps of contrasting papers as desired for patchwork

- Double-faced satin ribbon

**7.** Place the patterns on the wrong side of the appropriate papers, and mark as many of each piece as necessary. For each motif you will need one large center square and four of each remaining shape. You will need four additional small squares to fill in between the motifs (or as desired for your box).

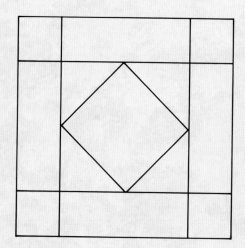

**8.** Glue the motifs to the box top as follows; complete one entire motif before beginning the next. Brush rubber cement over one outlined square on the box top. Brush rubber cement on the wrong side of the pieces for one patchwork motif. First place the four small corner squares inside the corners of the outlined square, then place the long side pieces. Next, place the triangular pieces; finally, place the large square in the center.

**9.** Glue small squares between the completed motifs.

**10.** Place the lid on the box. Wrap with ribbon and tie a simple bow over one corner as shown.

# PAIRED PACKAGES

*When you are giving more than one gift to the same person, consider wrapping each piece separately and tying them together in groups of two or three. Use this idea to dress up small gifts such as soaps or cosmetics, or even a set of books—your package will look more intriguing than a basic box. The paper and embellishment you choose could be elegant, like those shown here, or childlike or funky—whatever suits your whim.*

**1.** Following the directions for the seamless wrap on page 8, wrap each gift in white tissue, and then in gold or silver tissue.

**2.** Cut a strip of contrasting tissue long enough to wrap and overlap around one gift and a little wider than desired; fold the excess under on the long edges. Wrap the strip around the gift and secure it on the bottom with tape. Repeat for the other gifts.

**3.** Wrap a length of narrow ribbon around each gift, perpendicular to the tissue band, and knot on the bottom. Trim excess ribbon.

**YOU WILL NEED**

• White tissue paper for underwrap

• Matte gold and silver tissue paper

• Gold-edged purple curling ribbon

• Sewing needle and thread

**4.** Stack the gifts and wrap with another length of ribbon. Wrap in the same direction as the tissue band and knot on top of the stack, leaving tails.

**5.** To make a tissue flower for the top, cut a 2″ square of tissue in the same color as the base wrap. Place it wrong side up, then fold each corner to the center. Pinch and twist the center to make a cup shape (with the corners on the inside.) Thread the needle, wrap the pinched section several times with thread, then slide the needle through the knot of the ribbon on top of the package several times. Trim the excess thread. Curl the ends of the ribbon. (If your gift is larger than soap you might like to make the flowers larger, or make several for each package top.)

# RECYCLED CORRUGATED PAPER PACKAGING

*The corrugated paper packing inside the cartons of cosmetics, wine, or fragile food products can often be turned inside out to make handsome wrappings. Frequently tan or white, the corrugated material sometimes comes in lovely colors such as the soft green shown here. The corrugated texture lends itself to natural ties such as raffia strands with dried flowers, leaves, or even a starfish for decoration.*

## YOU WILL NEED

• Pieces of corrugated paper • Tissue paper • Raffia • Assorted dried leaves, flowers, or other natural adornments

**1.** Wrap the gift in tissue paper since it may show at the ends or sides of the corrugated paper.

**2.** Wrap the corrugated paper around the gift and tape in place with double-stick tape.

**3.** Wrap raffia around the gift and tie it in a knot or bow.

**4.** Tuck dried decorations under the raffia or affix them with craft glue.

# FLOWER-BOW WRAP

*To create an easy but especially pretty gift wrap, just choose a lovely paper, wrap the box, and top it with a lush, tendril-embellished bow—you do not really need anything more.*

**YOU WILL NEED**

• White tissue paper for underwrap • Rose-printed tissue paper • Ivory moiré ribbon, 1 1/2" wide • Floral wire

• Pink and yellow curling ribbon, 1/2" wide

**1.** Following the directions for the seamless wrap on page 8, wrap the box first in white and then in printed tissue.

**2.** Pass the moiré ribbon twice around the box (over each side) and tie in a square knot on the top. Cut the excess ribbon at the edge of the top and notch the ends.

**3.** Slide a length of pink ribbon from one corner of the top to the diagonally opposite corner, then secure it to the paper under the knot with double-stick tape. Repeat with another length in the opposite direction. Curl the ends of the ribbon.

**4.** Following the directions on page 11, make a twist bow from the moiré ribbon; attach it to the knot on the top of the box with floral wire.

**5.** Split several lengths of the curling ribbon into two or three thinner pieces. Place them under the wire, then pull them up through the loops of the bow. Curl the ends.

# DOILY DECORATED WRAPPINGS

*Paper doilies have the romantic aura of fancy pastries and the old-fashioned look of a linen tablecloth. They are available in a variety of shapes and sizes, are inexpensive, and are fun to decorate with cutouts or colored felt-tip pens. Heart-shaped doilies are great for Valentine's Day, and round, oblong, oval, or square doilies can grace wedding, shower, and housewarming gifts.*

## YOU WILL NEED

• Printed gift wrap or tissue paper   • Paper-backed fusible web   • Doilies   • Ribbon

**1.** Wrap the package with wrapping or tissue paper according to the directions for seamless wrap on page 8.

**2.** Select a motif from the wrapping paper such as the peach shown here, or cut out pictures from old greeting cards or magazine or catalog pages. When you cut out the motif, leave a margin of 1″ or so around it. Cut a piece of fusible web slightly smaller than the cutout. Iron the interfacing to the wrong side of the motif. Cut out along the edge of the motif. Peel off the protective paper and iron the motif to the center of the doily.

**3.** Cut small pieces of double-stick tape and place at each corner of the doily. Tape the doily to the package.

**4.** Tie ribbon bows around the package or glue them at the opposite ends of the doily.

**5.** Make a matching colored hang tag following the directions on page 11. Cut out a small piece of doily and glue it to the hang tag. Trim the edge of the tag just outside the edge of the doily. Tie it to the package with a thin strip of ribbon. (Curling ribbon can be split lengthwise into narrow pieces.)

# POMPOMS WITH TWISTED YARN TIE

*Yarn pompoms are a good way to use up odds and ends of knitting yarn and they can be recycled yet again to decorate ice skates or stocking caps, or to be used as toys for the family cat. The tie is made from twisting multicolored strands of yarn together.*

**1.** Cut two discs 2 1/4″ in diameter and two discs 1 1/2″ in diameter from the cardboard. Cut a notch about 1/2″ wide in each disc as shown.

**2.** Hold two matching discs together and wrap a double strand of yarn around the discs. Start wrapping next to the notch and continue until the yarn is several layers thick before moving on and wrapping the rest of the discs. Keep wrapping until the center hole is almost filled with yarn.

**3.** Thread the darning needle with a double strand of yarn. Combine two colors of yarn for a two-color pompom. With scissors inserted between the discs, cut through the yarn along the edges of the discs. When you have cut halfway around the discs, insert the darning needle between the discs, pull the yarn tightly around the center of the discs and knot it. Cut off the needle, leaving two yarn ends about 5″ long.

**YOU WILL NEED**

- Thin cardboard

- 3-ply knitting yarn

- Darning needle

**4.** Continue cutting the yarn around the edge of the discs. Remove the discs. Shake out the pompom and trim the longer ends until the pompom is sphere-shaped. Make several pompoms in the same way.

**5.** To make the twisted yarn ties, cut six lengths of yarn each 3 yards long. Mix colors as desired. Knot the ends of the strand together and tie them to a stationary object (a doorknob, or chair rung, for instance). Twist the yarn until it is tight. Hold the cut ends in one hand and pinch the center of the strands with the other hand. Hold the cut ends next to the ends tied to the doorknob and let go of the pinched center. The yarn will spin itself into a twisted cord. Knot each end tightly and cut off the excess. Wrap the cord around the package and tie it.

**6.** Tie the pompoms in a cluster and tie the cluster to the twisted tie on the package.

# DECOUPAGE BUCKET WRAP

*Here is a fun way to give fishing tackle to a young fisherman, or for that matter to one who is fully grown. Begin with a clean, empty bucket (recycle one that once held a citronella candle) and cover it with motifs cut from gift wraps or magazines—or use stickers. Pick a theme that reflects the gift or the interests of the recipient.*

**YOU WILL NEED**

• Bucket or other metal or plastic container  • Motif-printed paper or magazines  • Kneadable eraser  • Decoupage medium

• Sponge paintbrushes, 1/2" and 2" wide  • Tissue paper and shredded parchment to conceal gift

**1.** Cut out a number of motifs.

**2.** Arrange the motifs on the bucket as desired; use small bits of kneadable eraser as a temporary adhesive.

**3.** When your arrangement is complete, outline each motif lightly with pencil.

**4.** Remove the motifs one at a time, discarding the kneadable eraser. Brush decoupage medium onto the wrong side of the motif and reposition it on the bucket. Smooth out any air bubbles with your fingernail. When all the motifs are adhered, allow to dry.

**5.** Coat the entire bucket with decoupage medium, and let dry completely.

**6.** Line the bucket with appropriately colored tissue paper, hiding the gift between the layers. If desired, tuck shredded parchment into the tissue and let it trail over the edge of the bucket like seaweed.

# CORD AND TASSELS

*Sparkling tassels and twisted cord can be made from any metallic gift cord or mixed with silks or satin cord as shown here. Tassels may be bought already made or made from recycled materials, leftover metallic knitting yarn, used gift cord, or elegant embroidery materials. The cardboard gift tag has been embellished with a foil-covered chocolate coin glued in place with craft glue.*

## YOU WILL NEED

• Lengths of assorted cords  • Cardboard rectangle 2″ × 1 1/2″

**1.** To make a tassel, wrap the cord several times lengthwise around the piece of cardboard. Slip a separate piece of cord under the loops and tie it tightly in a knot. Slip the loops off the cardboard.

**2.** Holding the ends of the tie at the top of the tassel, wrap another short piece around the top of the tassel and tie it very tightly with a square knot. Dot craft glue on the knot. When the glue is dry trim the excess cord from the knot.

**3.** Cut the loops of the tassel and trim the ends evenly.

**4.** To make the twisted cord, cut several lengths of cord and follow Step 5 of the directions on page 48 for Pompoms with Twisted Yarn Tie.

**5.** Tie the tassel to the end of the twisted cord, or sew it to the cord with a needle and thread.

# FESTIVE KEEPSAKE WRAPS

*To make a keepsake box extra special, cover the top and bottom in coordinating seasonal paper, then add a fancy twist to the bow. The boxes shown are appropriate for the Christmas holiday, but you can easily interpret these designs with other papers and ribbons for other occasions.*

## THE TARTAN BOX

**1.** Wrap box following keepsake directions, page 9.

**2.** Wrap the box in each direction with a band of gold ribbon, securing the bands to each other with double-stick tape at the center of the top.

**3.** Cut a piece of tartan ribbon about 5″ longer than the longer edge of the box top, center it over the longer gold band, and affix it with double-stick tape.

**4.** Cut a piece of tartan ribbon about 6″ longer than the box is wide, center it over the shorter gold band, and affix it with double-stick tape.

**5.** Make two loops of gold ribbon slightly longer than the width of the box top. Cross them diagonally over the center of the top and affix with double-stick tape.

**6.** Make a tartan ribbon twist bow (see page 11) with seven wraps the width of the box top. Pinch and secure the center with tightly wrapped floral wire; spread the ends of the wire out flat under the bow and clip the excess about 1/2″ from the

### YOU WILL NEED

*for each wrap:*

- Sturdy box with separate lid
- Two coordinating decorative papers

*for the holly wrap:*

- Tartan wire-edged ribbon, 1 1/2″ wide
- Green curling ribbon, 1/2″ wide

*for the tartan wrap:*

- Translucent gold ribbon, 1 1/2″ wide
- Tartan wire-edged ribbon 3/4″ wide

twist. Adjust the loops to make a round, puffed shape. Secure the bow to the center of the box top with double-stick tape.

**7.** Notch and crimp the ends of the tartan streamers as desired.

## THE HOLLY BOX

**1.** Wrap box following keepsake directions, page 9.

**2.** Pass the tartan ribbon twice around the box (over each side) and tie in a square knot on the top; cut the excess, leaving tails that extend 2″ beyond the corners, and notch the ends.

**3.** Wrap two loops of tartan ribbon loosely around your hand, pinch them in the middle, and tie them to the box top with the tails left in the last step. Adjust and crimp the loops so the face of the ribbon is perpendicular to the box top. Crimp the tails.

**4.** Slide a length of green ribbon from one corner of the top to the diagonally opposite corner (under the knot) and secure it to the paper under the knot with double-stick tape. Repeat with another length in the opposite direction. Curl the ends of the ribbon.

# PAPER BAGS MADE PRETTY

*Colorful paper bags or plain old brown bags can become stylish totes for hard-to-wrap gifts such as small toys, socks, belts, or cookies, candies, and other food gifts. Foods will stay fresh longer if sealed in plastic bags inside the paper bags. This is also an inexpensive way to recycle odds and ends of ribbon left over from other gift wraps.*

## YOU WILL NEED

• Scraps of ribbon in various widths   • Hole punch

**1.** Cut lengths of ribbon three quarters of the height of the paper bag. Make the narrower ribbon slightly shorter than the wider ribbon. Cut V-shaped notches in one end of the ribbons. Glue the narrower ribbon in the center of the wider ribbon with rubber cement. Fold the top end of the ribbon over the top of the bag and glue it to the inside of the bag with craft glue.

**2.** Make the name tag according to the directions on page 11. Cover it with ribbon or paper and trim it to the desired shape and size. To tie the tag to the bag, punch a hole in the top or side of the bag with the hole punch and tie the cord through the hole.

**3.** To close the bag, roll the top over and seal it with double-stick tape.

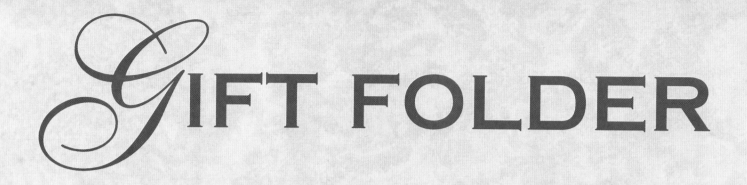

# GIFT FOLDER

*A special package for a lace wedding handkerchief (the traditional "something old," a family heirloom) is made from posterboard and fancy gift wrap paper. The butterflylike wings are part of the package and fold over to hook together to close. The edges are rimmed with glitter, and a satin bow with lilies of the valley is centered on the closure. Our package measures 6″ square for a standard handkerchief. You can make it larger for scarves or thin lingerie.*

## YOU WILL NEED

• Kraft paper, 14″ × 20″  • Posterboard, 14″ × 20″  • Masking tape  • Utility or matte knife with sharp blade and cutting mat  • Metal straight edge

• Glitter  • Silk lilies of the valley  • Satin ribbon

**1.** Photocopy and enlarge the pattern so that the dotted box measures 6″ on a side. Trace the pattern onto kraft paper and cut it out.

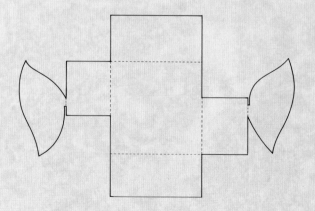

**2.** Cut a sheet of wrapping paper slightly larger than the posterboard. Spread rubber cement on the center third of the posterboard. Posterboard has one smooth side; spread the cement on the rough side. Starting at the center of the board, glue the wrapping paper down, smoothing out bubbles from the center toward the edges. Add rubber cement as you work from the center out to the ends.

**3.** Lay the pattern on the plain side of the posterboard and tape down the edges with masking tape.

**4.** Using a metal straight edge and matte knife cut along the lines of the pattern. Remove the pattern. Score lightly along the dotted lines on the plain side of the posterboard.

**5.** Fold along the scored lines.

**6.** Spread a bead of craft glue along the cut edges of the butterfly-shaped wings. Sprinkle glitter onto the wet glue. When glue is dry, shake off excess glitter. Add spots of glue and glitter to the centers of the lilies of the valley.

**7.** Tie a bow with the ribbon. Place the handkerchief or scarf in the package, fold the wings over, and hook them together. Glue the flowers and bow in place.

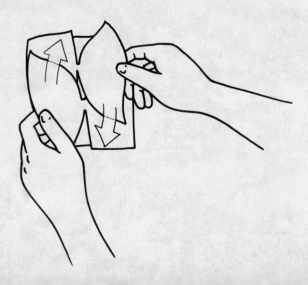

# SHOPPING BAG WRAP

*When you have a gift that simply won't fit in a box, wrap it up in tissue paper for protection, and put it in a decorated shopping bag. If you'd like to jazz this idea up, use a shiny bag and gild naturals with synthetic leaf, or use other materials such as feathers or lace, or even lollipops (especially if the recipient is a child).*

## YOU WILL NEED

• Brown paper shopping bag   • Assorted dried naturals: teasels, lavender, rosemary, bayberry, tansy   • Ecru curling ribbon

**1.** Arrange the dried naturals as shown or as desired and secure by wrapping in the center with floral wire. Tie a simple bow over the wire.

**2.** Position the arrangement on the bag to determine where it will be tied on. Mark these places lightly with pencil (except where you plan to tie around the handle).

**3.** Pierce the bag at each marked spot (through one layer only) with two holes about 1" apart; using the tips of scissors, cut the holes big enough to pass the folded ribbon through.

**4.** Cut an 8" length of ribbon, fold the end lengthwise to make a blunt point, and pass it through a pair of holes, leaving both tails on the outside. Repeat as needed. Tie the arrangement in place.

**5.** Place the gift in the bag. Tie the bag closed by tying ribbon around the base of the handles.

# WRAP FOR OVERSIZED CARTONS

Children's toys, small appliances, and winter clothing often call for big boxes that can be expensive and difficult to wrap with gift wrap paper. Kraft paper is durable and available in the larger widths needed for oversized cartons. Stencils, stickers, felt-tip pens, and crayons can be used to decorate these large blank spaces. Children's artwork is sure to please the artist and making it is a good way to occupy the kids before the birthday or holiday finally arrives.

**YOU WILL NEED**

• Kraft paper  • Posterboard for stencils  • Poster paints or acrylic paints  • Matte knife for adults, scissors for children  • Cellulose sponges

**1.** Wrap box according to the directions for the seamless wrap directions on page 8.

**2.** Draw stencil designs on posterboard with pencil. Cut out around the outside of the design leaving about 4″ as a margin. Cut out the center of the design.

**3.** Cut sponge into 3″ pieces.

**4.** Pour some paint on a plate and dilute with a little water if necessary. Dip the sponge into the paint and blot it on the plate. Hold the stencil on the box and pounce paint onto the kraft paper.

# FRUIT BASKET WRAP

When you see fruit displayed in a gourmet shop, each perfect piece is invitingly wrapped in colored tissue. If you

plan to give someone a gift of fruit—or any other edibles for that matter—you can easily do the same thing, and

present it in a basket. To give your basket a seasonal look, paint it with fabric dye (mix it following the

manufacturer's directions), and dye raffia to trim the basket as well.

## YOU WILL NEED

• Split oak basket, or as desired   • Printed tissue papers   • Fruit   • Nuts, spices, and cinnamon sticks for embellishment

**1.** Cut tissue paper into 6″ squares. If a square is badly creased, you can press it with a steam iron.

**2.** Wrap each piece of fruit with a tissue paper square, and arrange in the basket.

**3.** Embellish with nuts and spices as desired.

# STANDARD TIE OR GLOVE BOX

The standard tie or glove box is very simple to wrap but sometimes offers the opportunity to show off detailed gift

wrap papers to special advantage. Plan the arrangement of the paper's pattern on the box before you cut into it.

For instance, the bird pattern shown here is arranged so that the three main motifs are lined up on the top of the

box. Stripes, checks, and plaids can be run diagonally for added interest. Affix a large sheet of wrapping paper

to a window or glass-top table with masking tape. With light behind it, the pattern shows through to the wrong

side. Place the box on the pattern in the desired position and trace it lightly with a pencil. Take down the paper,

allow excess to wrap around the box, and then cut it away. Follow the directions for the seamless

wrap on page 8. This example has the added decoration of a small bird's nest, leaves, and

grasses glued to the ribbon surrounding the box.

# POTPOURRI BASKET WRAP

*When the gift itself is as beautiful and fragrant as an exotic potpourri, there is no reason to hide it—if your wrap is lovely enough,*

*the gift will be doubly appreciated.*

**1.** If desired, tint the cheesecloth by dipping it in hot coffee. Allow to dry.

**2.** Cut a piece of cheesecloth large enough to line and drape over the edge of the basket. Place it in the basket, arrange it as desired, and secure it with small ties of raffia.

**3.** Cut a square of gold tissue paper large enough to line and extend several inches above the top of the basket. Place it wrong side up in the basket, orienting the corners toward the ends if the basket is oval or oblong.

**4.** Cut two strands of raffia long enough to wrap twice around the basket. Tie them together at their midpoints. Place the knot in the bottom of the basket and extend the tails so one lies over each side of the basket (over the corners of the tissue).

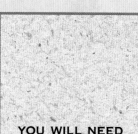

**YOU WILL NEED**

- Shallow basket

- Cheesecloth, enough to line basket and wrap potpourri

- Raffia

- Matte gold tissue paper

- Potpourri

**5.** Cut a large square of cheesecloth. Mound the potpourri in the center and tie the adjacent corners together over it to make a loose bag; cut off any excess cheesecloth. Invert the basket.

**6.** Tie the raffia tails over the center of the potpourri bag.

**7.** Fold each of the extending tissue corners into soft rosettes as follows, but do not make sharp creases. Fold the tip down to meet the potpourri, then fold the upright edges one over the other toward the inside of the basket; pinch and tie with raffia to secure the bud shape.

# GIFT TAG TEMPLATES

Below are some templates that can be used to make stylized gift tags for any occasion. Simply photocopy this page and cut out the tag of your

choice. Using pens or paints, decorate the photocopied tag and glue it to a piece of card stock; trim excess card stock.

Following the instructions on page 11, use a coordinated wrapping paper to cover the back of the tag.

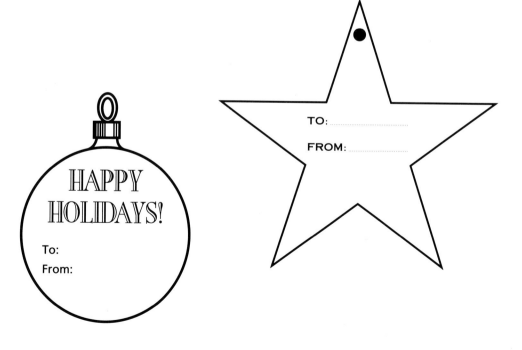

*Best Wishes*

**To:** _____

**From:** _____

*Congratulations!*

To:

From:

HAPPY
HOLIDAYS!

To:

From:

TO: _____

FROM: _____

*To:* _____

*From:* _____

HAPPY
BIRTHDAY!

to: _____

from: _____

*To:*
*From:*

# INDEX